Make
Meaningful
Work

DANIEL SZUC & JOSEPHINE WONG

Copyright © 2021 by Daniel Szuc and Josephine Wong

All rights reserved. Including the right of reproduction in whole or in part in any form.

Cover Design by: Derek Black
Artwork and illustration by: Huang Cheuk Ying
Editor: Dr Jin Peh

ISBN: 978-1-7379282-0-1
Kindle Direct Publishing

THANK YOU

Thank you to our family, friends and colleagues who have supported us over many years as we explore how we can Make Meaningful Work together.

This book is dedicated to Jo's Dad, our Ba.

contents

Thank you	
Foreword	i
How to apply this book	ix
Who this book is for	x
00 Our Story	**01**
Introduction	02
The groundwork behind Make Meaningful Work	07
Problems with typical training solutions	10
The Make Meaningful Work Learning Platform and Products	12
Outcomes	14
What it is and is not	16

01 Why Make Meaningful Work? — 19

21st century work problems	23
Ten key concepts to Make Meaningful Work	27
1. Insert meaning not finding meaning	27
2. Turn words into actions	30
3. Culture is the interactions and relationships between me and we	31
4. The Make Meaningful Work Sparkle Studio	33
5. Implicit practices in cultures at work	34
6. Practice Spotting™	36
7. Practice Spotting™ lenses to apply	37
8. Apply Practice Cards to Connect and Contextualise	39
9. Make time for structured explicit reflection and deeper understanding	41
10. Character building for sustainable learning and actionable impact	43
Sustained learning	45
Complimentary Online Learning Adventures for Make Meaningful Work foundations	47

02 Tools to Make Meaningful Work — 49

Practice Spotting™ Tool	52
7 steps to do Practice Spotting™	59
Practice Spotting™ in action	69
Make Meaningful Work Guided Practice Journal Tool	73
Complimentary Online Learning Adventures using tools to Make Meaningful Work	85

03 Sparkle Studio to Sustain Meaningful Work — 87

What is Sparkle Studio? — 88
Sparkle Studio in action — 89
Sustaining the Make Meaningful Work Sparkle Studio Community — 91
10 behavioural outcomes from the Sparkle Studio — 92

1. Enable Active Listening — 92
2. Build Awareness — 92
3. Spark Curiosity — 93
4. Solve Ambiguous Problems — 93
5. Foster Quality Relationships — 93
6. Contextual Adaptability — 94
7. Promote Diversity — 94
8. Navigate Complexity — 95
9. Build confidence — 96
10. Make Meaningful Decisions — 96

Multidisciplinary community — 97
Join our Adventures ahead — 98
Complimentary Online Learning Adventures to apply and sustain meaningful work — 99

How Make Meaningful Work has helped you? — 101
Appendix – Journaling Instruments — 107
About the authors — 117

Foreword

She was 5. In a moment of genuine curiosity, she changed the course of history. She created a pause, a moment so honest that it couldn't be anything but absorbed. She created meaning and she changed lives in an instant.

It was the dawn of a new century and I was a role player on a team of facilitators. We were consultants, venture capitalists, technopreneurs, skill trainers and coaches; all assigned to projects whose goal it was to help big organizations see their blind spots, develop new ways of working and move forward with bold new initiatives that weren't just profit-driven but were more holistic.

It was our biggest project to date and we had a full week with a new client (actually two) in the Silicon Valley facility. The goal was to help two massive oil companies merge, align and create a plan for their new future together.

Three days in and the process was working. Executives from both sides were finding common ground and devising cohesive strategies for capturing new market share, maximizing profits and satisfying concerned shareholders. All was good in the world of big oil.

As facilitators, we felt like it was going too smoothly. It was too easy. We needed to challenge them, make them uncomfortable, hit them with an angle they weren't anticipating. We began to dig through our "perturbation" strategies and landed on one that might do the trick.

We got the client group, nearly 160 of them together in the main space and gave them a challenge.

"We know it's only three days in, and it's 4 PM now, but tomorrow you must present all facets of your new business strategy, across all divisions, for every region in the world. You must have all your slides and materials ready to present to a live audience of investors and the public at 9 AM. Be ready to show us the new direction and really sell it to the world. This can't just be another big merger, how's this one going to change the game?"

The groans were audible, eye-rolls were everywhere and many of them were texting each other on their Blackberrys in disgust. They were paying us and the obvious feeling from them was this was not what they (as top tier executives) had signed up for. They just wanted to talk about the vision and not drill down to the brass tacks. This is what they pay others to do. Some of them even approached us to argue that we should save this exercise for the management retreat they were planning later in the year.

We held firm and they retreated to break-out spaces to start the deeper dive and prep work. They worked late into the night with the last team moving back to the hotel after 11 PM. A more honest effort than I expected and as facilitators, we were pleased. They seemed to be embracing the challenge, almost nostalgically remembering days when they did more of the gritty work.

That night we reset the space, documented the work from the day and made a few calls to enroll our audience for the morning.

A few minutes before 9 AM, the executives began rolling back in. One even bragged that they had outsourced their slideshow back to the main office and joked, "those poor saps must've been up all night trying to make us look good. We're ready for ya though. The audience is gonna wanna invest their money and their first born."

We welcomed the large group and sent them back to their break-out spaces for 30 minutes of final rehearsal. They acted like they didn't need it but grabbed coffees and pastries anyway as they meandered away. Just then, a bus pulled up to the back door. We greeted the guests and brought them into the main room for the presentations. They were excited about being with us. They were also five and a half years old. Two classes of them. 43 kids from a kindergarten down the street.

The audience sat anxiously as we prepped the executive teams in another part of the building. We asked which team would present first so we could prepare the tech and slides accordingly. The two CEOs thought it would be best for them to speak about the merger and the new shared vision first.

They had not asked a single question about who the audience would be.

The two CEOs remained backstage and the other division teams came to the main room and sat in the back. As they came in, they had different reactions to the kids sitting on the floor right up to the foot of the stage instead of sitting in the chairs we had set up. Most were polite to the kids and even gave a few high fives but all of them were looking at our team like we must have been joking.

The lights dimmed over the audience and the presentation lights came way up. The two CEOs came on stage from opposite sides to some motivational theme music they had chosen for the moment. This was their first moment to see the audience, some of whom were dancing and reaching up their hands to get a low five. Their faces could not hide the shock but they both laughed. As the music came down, the first words said by one of them were, "so it was all a joke eh? We knew you guys were just messing with us."

No one on our facilitation team said a word. The awkwardness set in and finally our tech team leader said over the mic, "please proceed with your presentation."

The first CEO had a look of acceptance on his face and immediately jumped straight into his presentation. The division teams clapped when they were supposed to and the CEOs started to play to their audience, behind the kids, making eye contact with only their own people on the outskirts of the room. The slides began to run in the background and then one little girl confidently shot her hand straight up into the air. The CEOs did not see her and as they continued, she became restless. She then knelt and began waving her hand wildly. Still unnoticed, she crawled closer to the stage and got on one knee, at one point literally pulling on the pant leg of the CEO who was not speaking at that time. Finally, they paused and asked her to stand. "Do you have a question for us, my friend?", one of them asked.

"Yes. I'm Maddy from Mrs. Jensens class."

She paused and looked around. Some of the adults clapped a bit and then the kids went wild.

Then, in a moment of total silence she asked, "Are you the people ruining the world?"

Both CEOs stepped backward. The room remained dead quiet. It seemed like an eternity. It was long enough to gain the sense that no one had put her up to this. She was not looking around for approval. She stood, chin lifted genuinely, eagerly awaiting an answer. It was pure childish curiosity.

One of the CEOs stepped forward. In a long pause, he looked around the room. It felt like he was trying to make eye contact with each person individually. Then he knelt down, directly in front of Maddy. He started to say something but immediately paused again. He finally pursed his lips and steadfastly looked her in the eye and said, "I don't want to be that person."

Maddy said, "thank you" and sat down with her legs crossed, both of them flapping like a grounded butterfly.

The room was still quiet.

Upon reflection, three things happened in that moment, all of which are the key to the kind of learning that drives change:

1. **Confrontation** – She stood up. Without bad intentions, but genuinely just asking out of curiosity. But she also needed that answer for her own comfort. They could have just said no and she probably would have just sat right down. But they couldn't because it landed and hit a nerve. There was an unavoidable truth, not in the question but in the moment of confrontation that everyone in that room had in their own heads and hearts where they had to say to themselves, "yes, I am ruining the world, but how can I convince you that I'm not?". It was a collective moment of shameful awkwardness. A noticeable wave of dropped heads, slumped shoulders, darting eyes and silence held the space. So powerful that it gut-punched everyone. They had to take a knee, acknowledge defeat, complete lack of preparation for this opponent and the realization that the real adversary was within.

2. **Contextualization** – No amount of corporate speak could justify what they did, who they are to a five year old. It forced them to her world view, looking back on themselves and they did not like what they saw. Context matters. Even if they were making money, pleasing shareholders, and dominating their market, they could not face a child

3. **Shift** – Something moved. Something clicked. A light bulb went on. Whatever you want to call it, there

was no going back. Everyone had experienced that moment together and its power was undeniable. Brushing her off would have made themselves a farce. They had to change. It was the only option. They were now feeling a mandate, driven by their own values and their own self-awareness. That little girl had triggered a new direction.

For the remainder of that week, the group was driven, collaborative, creative and self-directed. As facilitators, we did almost nothing other than help to capture the work. They instantly achieved a flow like state and their motivations were intrinsic. It was now personal. It mattered. Their shift was meaningful and they were loving it.

So, you can wait till a five year old embarrasses you in front of your fancy friends or you can start to do the work, the meaningful work that keeps you aware, alert to challenges, obstacles, opportunities, relationships, resources and the paradigms of yourself.

That's what MMW does. It keeps you from sleepwalking, stumbling through work without purpose, relationships without human connection and success without meaning. The MMW tools and community will provide you with these three critical things:

Confrontation – Take a look at yourself, acknowledge what is not working and hold yourself accountable.

Contextualize – Look at the places, situations and relationships in your life where there is room for improvement and then commit to making it so.

Shift – Take action by identifying specific practices to apply immediately and progressively to sustain change, learning and growth.

At the core of MMW is the belief that learning requires engagement. The ultimate tool is going to be your ability to direct your own process of learning, and self-discovery. MMW will provide you with all the tools to make that happen.

The MMW tools are elegantly simple and iterated over so much practice and research that they just work intuitively. They will accelerate your growth to insert meaning in all that you do.

Greg Evans, Founder, Seeds Training

How to apply this book

We suggest to apply the book as follows:

Try the complimentary online Learning Adventures at the end of each chapter after you read about the fundamentals.

Gain an overview of the Make Meaningful Work framework and then apply the tools to your own projects at work.

Attend the online Make Meaningful Work Shows in conjunction with the self directed online Learning Adventures.

Set up your own team's or organisation's Make Meaningful Work Sparkle Studio, and use this book for some of the fundamentals to kick off that plan.

Who this book is for

Individuals who:

- Feel like you are sleepwalking from time to time

- Don't want another process and tools that are hard to apply when the Make Meaningful Work framework and tools can be plugged into existing processes.

- Are curious about a simple way of encouraging self directed learning and practice, and sustaining transferable soft skills that we call practices.

- Are stuck in work or life and would like to try something straightforward to help them reflect and take appropriate actions.

- Would like to widen their perspectives.

- Have tried to change their team or organisational culture and feel overwhelmed as changes have not been sustainable.

- Are looking for a learning and development program that is easy to start with and more contextually relevant to their current workplace.

- Would like a multidisciplinary team to work together more effectively to cultivate and reiterate the culture they are aiming for.

- Already have an existing knowledge base, so that the Make Meaningful Work framework and tools can help them to connect and contextualise this knowledge, allowing them to reflect on, practice, record and action practices immediately.

Groups including but not limited to:

- **Chief Executive Officers and their management reports** – focusing on both the organisational strategy and developing a culture that enables potential that we describe as Sparkle.

- **Human Resources** – focusing on programs that offer ways to develop people professionally.

- **Program, Product and Project Management** – focusing on the design and development of humane products, services and experiences that serve a need for people and their environments.

- **Teams of designers and researchers** – focusing on the platforms upon which organisations build their products, services and strategies to guide production and its direction.

- **Educators, advisors, coaches, mentors and professional support** – focusing on providing spaces for professional structured explicit reflection and guidance to improve and sustain continuous learning.

This generally includes:

Individuals who seek:

- Customised learning to suit their roles and outcomes.
- Opportunities to grow in a structured manner.
- Lite programs that do not take too much time.

Teams who want to:

- Promote interdisciplinary ways of working and learning together.
- Connect to a vision, mission and values in practice.
- Provide access to mentors to help mature cultures at work.

Organizations who wish to:

- Attract and retain talent.
- Promote roles and outcomes based learning and development platforms.
- Sustain learning and development programs that lead the way forward.

修身、齐家、治国、平天下

【原文】

古之欲明明德於天下者,先治其國;欲治其國者,先齊其家;欲齊其家者,先修其身;欲修其身者,先正其心;欲正其心者,先誠其意;欲誠其意者,先致其知;致知在格物。物格而後知至,知至而後意誠,意誠而後心正,心正而後身修,身修而後家齊,家齊而後國治,國治而後天下平。

Improve yourself first, then you will be able to manage your family, then you will be able to govern your state, then peace and prosperity will come to the country.

Confucius talked about how a ruler should better manage his family and state through education, study & self improvement.

Where everything starts from self.

The famous phrase is actually a short version of a longer paragraph from "Book of Rites - Great Learning".

And the original goes like this:
"From ancient times, those who want to promote great virtue to the world, first need to govern their states; in order to govern their states, they need to first manage their family; in order to manage their family, they need to first improve themselves; in order to improve oneself, they need to regulate their mind; in order to regulate their mind, one needs to maintain sincere intention; in order to maintain sincere intention, one needs to exhaust one's knowledge; in order to exhaust one's knowledge, one needs to study the essence of the physical world.

Study the physical world, learn everything you can learn, be sincere with your intentions and regulate your mind; with your mind at the right place, you'll be able to improve yourself.

After you improve yourself, you can manage your family, after your family is managed, you can govern your states and bring justice and virtue to the World."

ch. **00** 01 02 03

our story

02 Introduction
07 The groundwork behind Make Meaningful Work
10 Problems with typical training solutions
12 The Make Meaningful Work Learning Platform and Products
14 Outcomes
16 What it is and is not

Introduction

Everyone at some time can get lost in the noise, speed, and delivery of day-to-day work. We might even forget why we are working on a project in the first place.

This can result in feeling frustrated, purposeless, stressed and unhealthy.

Distractions can shift our focus away from project tasks that we need to complete to achieve meaningful outcomes. They also create environments and cultures in which we might fall prey to transactional practices that leave us little room to pause, take stock and reflect on what is most important: the work that we are doing together and how we interact and relate with each other while doing that work.

We can all feel stuck at times.

We call this **Sleepwalking.**

Almost ten years ago, we also felt stuck in our work and experienced sleepwalking.

So we decided to take a break with our friends Bas and Geke to visit the pandas in Chengdu in China. This gave us the time for conversations and explicit reflection. It also inspired all of us to the possibilities of learning and development.

This explicit reflection time helped us to provide some clues and direction on what eventually became the Make Meaningful Work project that you will read about in this book. The intention of this book is to give readers an idea of the thinking behind the Make Meaningful Work framework. It also introduces the Make Meaningful Work tools to you.

This is not just about content delivery. It will allow you to turn words into actions where the Make Meaningful Work tools and community will help you sustain your actions.

As we conducted research for this book and framework, we listened to stories globally and observed the following about people at work:

- Feeling busy and stressed.
- Not engaged at work.
- Do not know how to address or cope with bad behaviour.
- Catching up with never ending tasks.
- Lacking meaningful interactions or relationships with coworkers.
- Working unnecessarily long hours.
- Feeling anxious and being unwell mentally and physically.

- Not connected to their own sense of meaning in their work and in a greater meaning beyond their role.

- Not connected to their organisational values, purpose, mission and vision.

- Not aware of healthy practices needed for today's work.

- Not adopting healthy practices or practicing them in a regular and rigorous manner.

- Not taking the time to stop and reflect on their work by stepping away from transactional work.

- Lack a structured way to record and learn from their experiences.

- Not tracking potential and improvement through the use of healthy practices.

- Not connected with team and organisational cultures.

- Lack deep or meaningful relationships with colleagues.

- Feeling lost and helpless.

- Not contributing to something that agrees with the mission.

- Cannot connect the tasks with the strategy or mission.

- Frustrated with bad behaviour or culture in teams and do not know what to do to confront it.

We discovered that most of us want to spend more time on meaningful work and work with teams that are engaged in making that happen. Projects where our skills and practice strengths are working well together that encourage us to learn, improve and thrive.

We call this **Sparkle.**

So as you read this book consider this, what if we:

- Foster strong relationships with colleagues.//
- Do not need to quit our profitable job and work for non profit organizations to have meaning.
- Insert meaning into what we do.
- Explore multiple tempos for our project work, in which speed is not the predominant factor.
- Create intentional moments for people to practice and reflect on work that gives meaning.
- Enable everyone (independent of their role, function and discipline) to feel connected to a sense of purpose.
- Challenge assumptions (unless they are backed up by evidence), reducing unnecessary work and waste.
- Discover alternative responses to the usual "busy" with the question – "how is work?"

- Find the time and space to look ahead and reflect on the implications of what is happening right now.
- Take responsibility to create and shape our own work culture.
- Create a collective mindset and attitude that is aligned with shared goals to solve meaningful problems and achieve sustainable outcomes.

There are numerous studies aimed at finding how to make work more meaningful and how different workers find meaning. However, they do not provide a process for doing so consistently across different personalities, industries and job types. This has been our goal in writing this book.

The groundwork behind Make Meaningful Work

The "Make Meaningful Work" framework is inspired by workshops globally where we facilitated questions and answers on how we can Make Meaningful Work.

The groundwork includes a range of domains and industries such as financial services, education, media, logistics, ecommerce, insurance, utilities and hotels, just to name a few. This ensures that our framework works across a range of personalities, industries and cultures.

We covered:

1. Interviews, workshops and presentations to thousands of people globally to gain a clearer understanding of what work looks and feels like in their locales.
2. Expert inputs from a range of locations, industries, job roles, work experiences, cultures, work types and personal backgrounds.
3. Understanding local and global patterns in work places.
4. Presenting at conferences globally to look at the problems inside and outside of work.

5. Workshops with individuals and teams in organisations to collect stories and evidence to develop key elements of the Make Meaningful Work framework, tools and Sparkle Studio that inform our proposition and provide direction.

6. Desktop research including articles from hundreds of publications that cover business, innovation, leadership, change and transformation, digital, social science, psychology, philosophy, personal development, economics, sociology, engineering, design, art, linguistics, science, futures, Chinese philosophy, and traditional Chinese medicine.

7. Books on design, leadership, business, culture, innovation and change etc.

We also examined articles, books and films on Eastern and Western philosophy, and global conversations from diverse cultural backgrounds.

The current framework and tools are also the results of the Make Meaningful Work workshops that have enjoyed numerous conversations in the following locations: Hong Kong, Shenzhen, Beijing, Shanghai, Taipei, Singapore, Jakarta, Kuala Lumpur, London, Brighton, Norwich, Melbourne, Canberra, Sydney, Bangalore, Ottawa, Toronto, Seattle, Atlanta, Portland, Wellington, Auckland, Hobart, Vercelli, Bologna, Milan, Jönköping, Lisbon, Dallas, Boston, Los Angeles, San Francisco and New York.

To be able to "Reactivate your Potential" in a traditional Chinese medicine setting, it is critical to reactivate our natural healing system and strengthen our internal environment. This natural healing system is often damaged by what we do and what we eat.

In our societies and workplaces, we are in an environment that makes us think that we should behave in a certain way in order to fit in that often constrains our potential. We hope the Make Meaningful Work tools and community can facilitate you to reactivate your potential by using self directed learning and by practicing and cultivating capabilities to sustain the learning.

Problems with typical training solutions

- Focusing mainly on hard skills and using the same approach to soft skills.
- Focusing only on content delivery that is hard to relate.
- Dry content that is broadcasted and not engaging for the audience.
- Theories that are hard to apply in reality.
- Rare case examples that are unrealistic for most people.
- Practices that are hard to sustain in relevant roles at work.
- You are often passively receiving content, without the opportunity to rehearse the practices and apply them in context.

The Make Meaningful Work framework has been explicitly designed to address these issues. The framework and tools are easy to pick up, as we emphasize on learning how to connect and contextualise to your environment.

Once you learn how to use the tools, you can self direct what you want to learn by yourself and with others. You can be supported and motivated by your learning buddies and the community around you to grow together and take sustainable actions into context.

Make Meaningful Work focuses on the transferable soft skills that we call practices, as we cannot solve problems by just applying hard skills. The combination of applying soft skills in practice together with hard skills enables us to take responsibility and insert meaning into what we do.

The Make Meaning Work Learning Platform and Products

The following Make Meaningful Work (MMW) products form the MMW Learning Platform help "Reactivate your Potential":

- **MMW Book** – this book describes the why, the tools and the Sparkle Studio experience to apply MMW in your own work.

- **Practice Spotting™ Tool** – is an observational and sense-making tool to make the implicit practices explicit.

- **MMW Guided Practice Journal** – helps to explicitly reflect, practice, record and sustain practices and includes cards for : Character, Story, Notes, Spotting, Practice and Progress; and also includes a Learning Portfolio and Meaning Canvas.

- **MMW Sparkle Studio** – is a learning platform that is both physical and online. It encapsulates a fun practice and learning experience.

- **Learning Adventures** – online learning and development programs suitable for various audiences covering leadership, character building, team building and culture.

- **MMW Game** – is a game mixed with online tools to make the learning experience fun, memorable and practical to action as a take away.

- **MMW Shows** – is a series of shows that has guests from all over the world from different industries and disciplines.

This all forms part of the MMW global community.

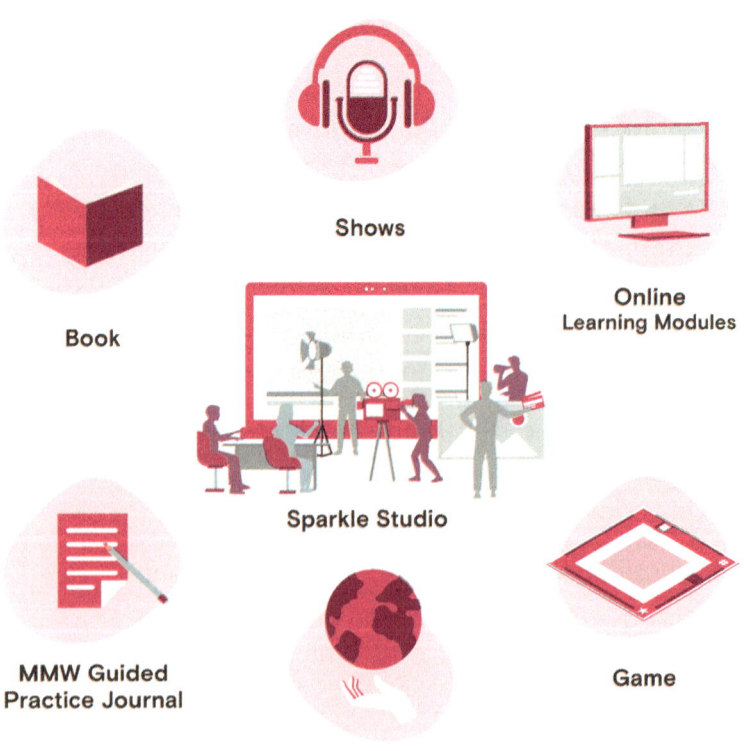

Make Meaningful Work Learning Platform

Outcomes

After integrating the Make Meaningful Work Learning platform into your existing process you will enjoy the following outcomes:

1. Use the Practice Spotting™ tool to turn implicit practices into explicit ones so that we know what you need to address or enhance.

2. Define a clear learning and development plan for transferable soft skills that we call practices.

3. Identify and continue using the practices that will build confidence and allow you to make meaningful decisions.

4. Use the Make Meaningful Work lenses to identify practice gaps.

5. Turn theories into actions with micro exercises that are contextualised and easy to practice.

6. Connect practices related to your role to apply and insert meaning immediately into your work.

7. Create, shape and rehearse the culture we want when organizations are aware of the desired behaviour.

8. Use the Make Meaningful Work Guided Practice Journal to record, reflect and track as we learn.

9. Develop and sustain actionable outcomes based on roles through continuous practice with various learning buddies.

10. Access Global Mentors to support the contextual needs and practice outcomes to Make Meaningful Work.

Make Meaningful Work is a triple win for individuals, organisations and society.

As you become more self aware by journalling and gaining your own perspectives, you will be able to make unlikely connections by seeing more dots. You become more reflective and see the blind spots that you may not have seen before. This helps you to challenge your assumptions and make meaningful decisions.

It also helps integrate the practices into your daily work by enhancing quality relationships, asking more questions, challenging ideas and reinforcing the importance of always getting better. This is part of your own growth and development.

What it is and is not

Consider the comparison on what Make Meaningful Work is and is not in the table below.

is ✓	is not ✗
A plug-in that is adaptable and complimentary	A one size fits all tool
Applying Practice Spotting™ to determine the practices you need in context	A method or formula that you can just passively follow
Connected and contextualised to your work and the Learning Adventures based on your specific needs	A fixed curriculum
Interconnected	A linear process or methodology
Half framework & half your own efforts to understand your context by applying Practice Spotting™	Just one framework disconnected from your context
Multiple options of implicit practices that we can apply at the same time	About right or wrong practices
Starting points based on needs and stress points	Binary with right or wrong answers and approaches
Based on different people in various contexts	Fixed contexts
Lifelong learning and practice	A graduation

You take responsibility for meaning to insert into relevant contexts for immediate action	You search for meaning
Practicing with others in the Sparkle Studio using the Make Meaningful Work Guided Practice Journal to improve through daily practice	A traditional training in a classroom setting
Facilitators are leaders, and learners are potential facilitators and leaders	One way teaching and learning

To Make Meaningful Work, we need to be intentional about what practices contribute to the wellness of people, work, projects, communities and economies that create an enlightened future. We hope that it will help us know ourselves better and reactivate our potential beyond our current perspectives and boundaries.

This book's tools will help you turn words into actions by:

- Learning how to spot practices needed for different roles.
- Learning how to connect and contextualize to your own situation.
- Practicing contextual micro exercises in your own time every day.

- Reflecting, recording, practicing, applying and tracking progress using the Make Meaningful Work Guided Practice Journal.

As we explore the Make Meaningful Work key concepts together, note the critical insights that overarch these concepts:

- Meaning is not something that you have to search for.
- Meaning is inside of you and you can transform that meaning from feelings into words and actions.
- The actions you choose and your daily choices will have a profound impact over time.

Learn More About Us

ch. 00 **01** 02 03

01 why*

- 19 Why Make Meaningful Work?
- 23 21st century work problems
- 27 Ten key concepts to Make Meaningful Work
- 45 Sustained learning

Why Make Meaningful Work?

We spend one third of our life working and yet most of us relate to work as just a job that is disconnected from our personal life. There are consequences for not enjoying work, not feeling engaged or being unfulfilled in what we do. This includes:

- Loss of confidence.
- Low self esteem.
- Accepting the status quo and templates handed to us.
- Having to comply with a misalignment of values.

In fact, some of us are so stressed and anxious that it negatively affects our immune system and leads to sickness. We also hear about people who try very hard to have a work life balance. But is a work life balance really the answer? If we spend one third of our life at work consumed by stress, do we really still have a life?

Some of us try to fix this by:

- Additional study of hard skills to gain and collect more certificates.
- Taking organisational training, retreats, team building programs, cultural transformation / change programs, organisational restructures, or wellness programs etc.
- Changing jobs or careers.
- Developing soft skills in the same way as learning hard skills.
- Converting knowledge into something concrete by reading books, articles, papers etc.

These fixes leave significant gaps:

- We often want quick answers and instant results.
- They focus on hard skills, rather than the transferable soft skills we desperately need to face challenges in the 21st century.

- Some theories are very hard to apply in real scenarios and contexts.

- There is a lack of safe spaces to reflect, practice and sustain the skills in a meaningful way.

- When we do practice reflections, we do not have the tools or structures to guide us.

- There is not a wider community to support us.

21st century work problems

We are facing a world where technology will continue to replace humans for many jobs, especially those that involve repetitive and programmable tasks. This creates uncertainties in our world and also has implications for our planet's future. Therefore, it is vital to rethink how we learn and adapt to new work environments.

We need to strengthen our creative and heart muscles. Organisations must prioritise upskilling in order to attract people that will grow and evolve. However, there may be gap problems with their skills. Traditional learning programs do not always understand the actual context in which gaps with skills are experienced. So we do not know the relevant practices and meaningful outcomes that relate to their specific work roles.

We are good at managing tasks, but not so good at managing ourselves as complex and unique people . Constantly delivering and focusing primarily on the transactional nature of work is not healthy. Such workplace cultures do not encourage explicit moments to stop, reflect, share stories, practice, learn and mature over time.

Our automatic mode of just doing without asking results in a lot of waste involving finances, time and intellect.

As we listen to people across the globe who share their project stories, these statements were universal and disheartening.

- I feel busy all the time.
- I don't have time to think or reflect.
- I feel stressed, tired and fatigued.
- I'm not healthy.
- I lack energy.
- I don't make time for learning and reading.
- I fake it until I make it.
- I don't feel connected to the organization's mission and values.
- I keep focusing on the wrong thing.
- I work at a quick pace just to work at a quick pace.
- I don't trust my colleagues.
- I feel stuck.
- I don't care about the quality of outcomes. I just want to get it done.
- I don't have any impact.

- I don't know why I am doing what I am doing.
- People around here just focus on themselves and not the collective good.
- No one recognises the good work that I have done.
- I feel I need to justify decisions with numbers and short term thinking.

And many more...

Typical solutions that we see:

- Training that often focuses on hard skills to boost productivity.
- Wellness programs that are bolted on instead of being embedded into our work.
- Yearly retreats which are hard to apply in context and not sustainable.
- Change management programs that focus on the process while ignoring the systemic patterns at play in work.
- Restructuring exercises that feel like simply moving the furniture around.
- Placing more processes on top of existing processes with the idea that the whole thing will result in a breakthrough.
- Key Performance Indicators (KPIs) that do not directly connect to a person's job and add complexity beyond the existing skill sets.

- Performance review systems that are disconnected from daily activities and lack any support for improvement.

- Heavy reliance on transferable soft skills that we call practices which are acquired implicitly over the years to deal with what is in front of you.

We do not recognise the importance of transferable soft skills and we do not have a structured way of spotting and acquiring these transferable skills we call practices.

Ten key concepts to Make Meaningful Work

In consideration of 21st century work problems, we defined ten key concepts to Make Meaningful Work to help you. These ten concepts will help you consider and apply the best practices that consider what we want 21st century work to look and feel like that will "Reactivate your Potential".

1
Insert meaning not find meaning

When we talked to people about Make Meaningful Work, their first reaction was often that this is a luxury as work is not meaningful. Meaning was defined as the need to quit a day job and work for a charity instead.

When we talk about meaningful work, we are talking about how individuals can insert meaning into what they do and into the interactions and relationships between people by not just focusing only on the task itself. There are different ways of doing a task with many different mindsets and attitudes.

Contextual micro exercises are recorded on Practice Cards to help you apply the practice in the relevant context. These are micro because they are not intended to be heavy or hard to do. Micro exercises build on the subsequent exercises that develop the practices, habits and culture you wish to see in your work.

You can insert meaning through action with any adventure that ultimately starts with you. We believe everyone is capable of inserting meaning into their work and life and in the tasks, activities and interactions with people, no matter how small. It is not about the task or activity itself. It is about how you behave in doing these tasks and how you humbly interact and relate with people, time and place.

"Man's Search for Meaning" Viktor E. Frankl

"What was really needed was a fundamental change in our attitude towards life.

We had to learn ourselves and furthermore we had to teach the despairing man that it did not really matter what we expected from life, but rather what life expected from us.

We needed to stop asking about the meaning of life, and instead to think of ourselves as those who were being questioned by life – daily and hourly. Our answer must consist, not in talk

and meditation but in right action and in right conduct.

Life ultimately means taking the responsibility to find the right answer to its problems and to fulfil the tasks which are consistently set for each individual.

These tasks, and therefore the meaning of life, differ from man to man, and from moment to moment. Thus it is impossible to define the meaning of life in a general way. Questions about the meaning of life can never be answered by sweeping statements.

Life does not mean something vague, but something very real and concrete, just as life's tasks are very real and concrete. They form man's destiny, which is different and unique for each individual. No man and no destiny can be compared with any other man or any other destiny.

No situation repeats itself, and each situation calls for a different response. Sometimes the situation in which a man finds himself may require him to shape his own fate by action. At other times it is more advantageous to make use of an opportunity for contemplation and to realise assets in this way"

—Viktor E. Frankl

"Man's Search for Meaning" by Viktor E. Frankl

2
Turn words into actions

Most of us generally have good intentions at work and want to contribute positively. Mostly, we have good intentions and are able to convert the intentions into words that relate to our work outputs.

However, it is very hard to transfer the words into actions with the positive impact that we want. Often, we have different interpretations and perceptions about the words and form discrepancies between words and actions. Value, or meaning is often hidden between words and actions in what we call the gap. This includes the environment or culture in which elements of our work live such as language, process, conversations, methods, values, beliefs, motivations, and philosophies.

「行是知之始；知是行之成」陶行知

A Chinese educator Tao Xingzhi believes that:

"Practice/Do is the start of knowledge, Practice/Do is the completion of knowledge"

Tao Xingzhi believes in the cycle of do, learn and do again.

The gap is from the words to actions and impact.

We do not always explicitly observe and become aware of the practice gaps. We may not have the tools to record what is happening. We may not have practices that aid understanding of our own actions and intentions, as well as for others.

When we do Practice Spotting™ we are looking for practices that are implicit in nature. We then make them explicit by calling them out and recording the practice on a Practice Card. They become visible to all and allow us to take the steps to practice the contextual micro exercises.

The most important aim in the Make Meaningful Work framework is to sustain what we learn by practicing the micro exercises and insert meaning into what we do.

3
Culture is the interactions and relationships between me and we

An important dimension of culture is the interactions and relationships between the individuals (me) and teams and organisations (we). So by default, we are a critical part of a work environment where it is important to be able to spot practices to define and to know what we want the culture to be.

Our interactions and relationships between people at work is critical, no matter how small they are. These can have positive or negative impact over time as the micro interactions directly influence the relationships between people. This can have a big impact on how we work together.

Consider the microinteractions and behaviours in the moments between people. You can understand the impact they have on you and the people around you.

These microinteractions and behaviours include words and actions, such as taking the time to listen, acknowledging your colleagues, recognising good work, showing encouragement and support, saying thank you, or offering the courtesy of allowing another person to go first.

These microinteractions and behaviours can also be negative, such as sighing repeatedly around the people you work with.

Most of us want to perform good work that creates a positive impact. Very few of us want to deliberately sabotage projects or create toxic environments; they are just not aware of what they are doing.

We believe everything starts with me and extends to the we. Using Practice Spotting™ and other Make Meaningful Work tools, such as the Make Meaningful Work Guided Practice Journal, we can help you become more aware of how you and others behave. You can then enhance the positive behaviours through structured explicit reflection, practice, recording of practices and supporting each other to create the culture you want now.

4
The Make Meaningful Work Sparkle Studio

The Make Meaningful Work Sparkle Studio is a space (physical or online) that encapsulates a fun and practical learning experience. It allows you to learn how to connect the theories and contextualise them into daily micro exercises.

We need to learn transferable soft skills or practices differently from the way we learn hard skills. This is a space to shape and rehearse the culture you want for your team and organisation. It encourages:

- Cross disciplinary collaboration.
- Diversity and inclusion.
- Social and emotional learning.
- A supportive community.

In the Make Meaningful Work Sparkle Studio, we learn about relevant practices through playing different roles using the Make Meaningful Work tools. Through playing different roles, you get to experience a range of practices. You can then use the relevant practices to connect and contextualise into your specific role.

You can setup your own Make Meaningful Work Sparkle Studio with minimal effort and use Practice Spotting™ to drive the culture you desire by helping people to move from being to becoming by:

- Turning words into actions.
- Recording the actions into Practice Cards relevant to your roles.
- Practicing relevant micro exercises.
- Conducting regular facilitated studio sessions to create the desired sustainable culture.
- Checking the culture regularly without waiting for annual or bi-annual reviews.
- Creating a plan to reflect and project forward.

5
Implicit practices in cultures at work

Have you wondered why certain organisations that you worked for have toxic cultures and others have cultures that you enjoyed more so than others?

Or do you feel that there is something subtle happening with our own behaviour and that of others that makes you feel comfortable or uncomfortable but you just don't know why?

These subtle events are in play all the time and this is what we call Implicit practices.

Implicit practices are subtle behaviours that you do but do not think about. It is like muscle memory but you are doing it all the time. It is learned and used implicitly throughout our lives. These could be soft skills, mindsets, attitudes, values, thinking habits etc.

Many of us learnt the implicit practices implicitly throughout our lives from our parents, teachers, friends, colleagues and bosses, to name a few.

These subtle implicit practices have a significant and important impact on our behaviours, interactions and relationships with others.

Work culture impacts all of our behaviour: how you treat people, how others treat us, how we and they contribute to it. We need to understand how we want to behave and embody the practices to help support these behaviours.

6
Practice Spotting™

Practice Spotting™ is an observational and sensemaking tool that enables you to widen and deepen perspectives and challenge your assumptions to uncover the implicit practices. It uncovers the hidden learning opportunities from people in your life, the stories you hear, the books and articles you read, the films and videos you watch and the conversations you have.

Practice Spotting™ is a mindset or way to acquire knowledge to help see what is under the surface. It also lets you see what is really happening from both positive and negative perspectives. It helps us to break down observations into granular pieces. This allows us to connect and contextualise themes by creating practices and micro exercises as recorded in Practice Cards. As a result, we can practice more explicitly and insert meaning into what we do.

Practice Spotting™ opens our senses and helps us become more aware of ourselves and our environment. It allows us to recognise our blind spots and assumptions, thereby adding dimensions to what we see.

When you do Practice Spotting™, you are looking for behaviours that are implicit in nature. The intention is then to make them explicit by calling them out and recording them on a Practice Card so that they are visible to all. It helps make the implicit practices explicit and inserts meaning into what you do.

Practice Spotting™ helps deconstruct behaviours in environments made up of people, time and place. Practice Spotting™ helps us understand the larger narratives and know where to adapt, fit in and insert meaning in various environments and conditions.

When we have wider and more diverse perspectives, it helps us to connect the dots and make meaningful decisions.

7
Practice Spotting™ lenses to apply

Everyone has biases. We develop blind spots over time that limit our perspectives. So if we can be more aware of our biases and blind spots, we can counteract them and stop them from holding us back.

Lenses are applied during Practice Spotting™ to help us look at stories and contexts from different dimensions. Starter lenses can include enablers and barriers to help us look at moments from different people's views or from a particular moment of time. This helps to ensure we do not become biased too quickly in our understanding of people, time and place. It also helps to ensure a selection of the relevant practices we may need for a specific context.

You can use as many lenses as you want or need. These different lenses will help you to expand and add perspectives, determine where to focus, uncover how you feel, identify where the noise exists and where you may need to better focus. They also encourage individuals, teams and organisations to take enough time for structured explicit reflection and pursue ideas or practices that pique their curiosity. These include the following four lens groupings:

1. Attitude and mindset – open or closed.
2. Perspectives and opportunities – past, present and future.
3. Communication and intent – individual and team outcomes.
4. Impact and time – success based on commitment.

To help us gain perspectives to see more widely and reduce biases and blind spots, we can:

- Listen to other people's perspectives.
- Probe to see what we may not immediately see.
- Zoom out to gain greater perspective.

- Zoom in on the details within the bigger picture.

Then, we can share and clarify our perspective by:

- Confronting the issues to help solve problems.
- Connecting the dots to gain focus.

Finally, we can iterate on the meaningful actions we need to take based on our perspectives by:

- Knowing what we need to work on and why.
- Prioritizing what work to focus on now.
- Focusing on that work and its meaning.

8
Apply Practice Cards to Connect and Contextualise

When we learn at school or in training, the knowledge is usually not connected with our own context. In traditional learning, we are given exercises to complete that do not relate to your context and needs.

In Make Meaningful Work, you need to come up with your own contextualised micro exercises, so they can be useful, practical and relevant to your needs right now.

Even if we are taking the same Learning Adventures, the practices that interest you and I may be different. Additionally, the micro exercises in your Practice Card and mine will most definitely be different because we all need to connect the practices and contextualise the exercise into our own work and projects.

When you create Practice Cards, you need to select practices you feel are relevant and connected to your context. These practices may be:

- Something you are already skilled in.

- Something you would like to strengthen and enhance over time.

- Recognising a practice gap that you think needs to be improved.

- A practice that you would like to pay more attention to when you are doing Practice Spotting™ and completing your Spotting Card.

When we use Practice Cards together with contextual micro exercises that result from Practice Spotting™, we can use these practices and exercises. They directly connect and contextualise to the environment and work cultures in a relevant manner.

The key is that you come up with the micro contextual exercises that are connected to your own context so they will be practical and useful.

9
Make time for structured explicit reflection and deeper understanding

Many of us know that reflection is very important. However, we do not always have the structures, tools and support to reflect effectively which then allows us to take contextual actions immediately. We need Make Meaningful Work to create the spaces in which we can reflect and practice together safely.

When we slow down and take the time to reflect, we also consider the proper perspectives and the implications of continuous learning. As a result, we can then adopt the relevant practices to help us perceive intersections. We can see the dots we have to connect as circles that intersect with each other. When people with diverse backgrounds and disciplines meet at these intersections, they have to develop a shared language. To find the magic at these intersections, they have to share the common intention to Make Meaningful Work.

Structured explicit reflection, as a practice, allows you to assess the interactions that occur during your project work. It also lets you consider how well your environment is supporting you in your work and whether you have the practices you need to truly Make Meaningful Work. Such reflection highlights the gaps and areas where you need to learn and to consider who can support you in remedying specific practice deficiencies.

This is not just about finding out who you are, but also about building on micro decisions to support who you want to be. This then allows you to actively contribute to self development and to the development and potential of others.

Spending a moment each day examining the potential for a project's significance through structured explicit reflection and Practice Spotting™ helps us to :

- Be caring, compassionate and flexible and connect the dots.
- Not fall into the trap of thinking in absolutes.
- Be a curious, generous and life-long learners.
- Evolve local and global perspectives to enhance diversity and to think beyond the status quo

Taking the time to reflect with a buddy is an excellent way to learn together through sharing stories, doing Practice Spotting™ and identifying contextual micro exercises to practice. Reflecting with a buddy also helps you to look at the stories and contexts in the stories through different lenses. This allows you to gain access to different perspectives.

The practice of structured explicit reflection affords us moments that encourage the practice of curiosity, prompting new thinking that will inform a better future and make meaningful decisions.

10
Character building for sustainable learning and actionable impact

Character refers to the values and moral qualities that act as our inner compass. Since character is something that is inside of us, we do not pay much time or explicit attention to nurture, build and shape character.

In Make Meaningful Work, we believe everything starts with me as the individual and extends to a bigger collective in the we.

The term character building implies we are taking the time to build up our sense of self. We also consider how this connects to the cultures at work. They consist of the interactions and relationships between people, time and place.

Character building helps us to better understand ourselves as characters, as well as the characters of the people we work with. Supported by the Character Card in the Make Meaningful Work Guided Practice Journal, we can connect and contextualise with others via the collective stories, practices and outcomes. The Make Meaningful Work Character Card is intended to help you build your character by enabling you to add dimensions and depth to reflect on and project forward the qualities you want for your character.

Sustained learning

Traditional learning is hard to sustain in a practical context after we acquire the necessary skills. Athletes spend thousands of hours practicing the fundamentals needed to do advanced routines. Using the Make Meaningful Work framework and tools, the major proportion of this is to facilitate and support sustained learning through:

1. Micro exercises you create for the context you need it in.

2. Tools like Practice Spotting™ and the Make Meaningful Work Guided Practice Journal.

3. A buddy to practice and reflect with so you have the support to continue.

4. A global community you can connect with and rely on to get mutual support.

This is a continuous journey that we need to take one step at a time. There is no one magic template that you can use. Continuous learning creates flexibility and fluidity in our work. We must have moments when we can reflect on which practices speak to us, identify our practice strengths, and more importantly, recognize any practice gaps.

We need more moments in our work when we can consider the data we have gathered. This includes the short-term implications of our observations and also what they will mean in the long term. We must consider what questions we need to ask and consider the answers. There will be implications for roadmaps, lives, and how our work impacts the work of others.

To sustain the learnings we can:

- Practice micro exercises that are not totally new to us for an easier start.

- Use micro exercises that are connected to your own contexts so it will be practical, useful and relevant to you.

- Practice with a buddy so that you can reflect on and support each other.

- Reflect and receive support from the global Make Meaningful Work community.

Complimentary Online Learning Adventures for Make Meaningful Work foundations ———————

Here is a complimentary Adventure Card and practices you can try out for yourself:

⚜ Learning Adventure Card

Active listening to build awareness

- **Active listening**
- Build awareness
- Sensing

Take the online Learning Adventures here

ch. 00 01 **02** 03

02
tools

49	Tools to Make Meaningful Work
52	Practice Spotting™ Tool
59	7 steps to do Practice Spotting™
69	Practice Spotting™ in action
73	Make Meaningful Work Guided Practice Journal Tool

Tools to Make Meaningful Work

Consider this:

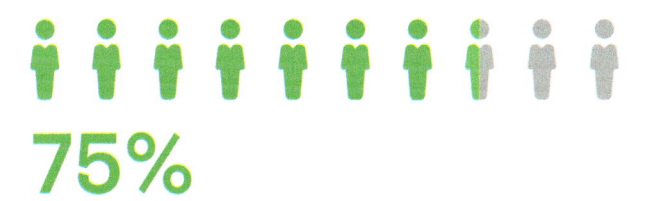

75%

of 1,500 managers surveyed from across 50 organizations were dissatisfied with their company's Learning & Development (L&D) function.

70%

of employees report that they do not have mastery of the skills needed to do their jobs

x 150 managers

Where Companies Go Wrong with Learning and Development
by Steve Glaveski

Organisations focus on training people on hard skills but on the other hand employees put heavy reliance on transferable soft skills that we call practices. These transferable soft skills are acquired implicitly over the years to deal with problems they are facing in their jobs. We do not recognise the importance of implicit practices (transferable soft skills) and we do not have a structured way of spotting and acquiring these implicit practices.

So we need a tool to help us learn how to spot the implicit practices and make explicit reflections, learn and develop self directed learning practices. A tool that encourages us to "connect and contextualise" the practices and insert meaning into what we do in a sustainable manner – this is the driving goal of the Practice Spotting™ Tool.

Practice Spotting™ Tool

Practice Spotting™ is an observational and sensemaking tool that enables you to widen and deepen perspectives and challenge your assumptions to uncover the implicit practices. It also uncovers the hidden learning opportunities from people in your life, the stories that you hear, the books and articles that you read, the films and videos that you watch and the conversations that you have.

We developed this tool as we observed individuals, teams and organisations at work to:

1. Be more aware of the behaviours of the self and others.
2. See what the implicit and explicit practices are around you.
3. Uncover the practices that you want to strengthen.
4. Embody the explicit interactions and behaviours you want to promote in yourself, team and organisation.
5. Take ownership of learning, practice and sustain the implicit practices (transferable soft skills) to promote the culture that we desire.

It is critical to be aware of and understand our own behaviour (and that of others) in the context of any particular environment with its inherent culture. This improves our internal and external environment. Our environment includes the place in which we work, the people with whom we work, the culture of our workplace, and even our colleagues' and shareholders' emotions. All of these factors can help or hinder our ability to make a meaningful impact.

Consider the microinteractions and behaviours in the moments between people and their impact on you and others. These microinteractions and behaviours include words and actions such as taking the time to listen, acknowledging your colleagues, recognising good work, showing encouragement and support, saying thank you, or offering the courtesy of allowing another person to go first. These microinteractions and behaviours can also be negative such as sighing repeatedly around the people you work with.

Our interactions with people in a workplace is critical no matter how small they are.

Practice Spotting™ helps us gain clarity on what is happening within the environments we experience. A person's environment comprehends both what is within and outside that individual.

Practice Spotting™ can help you to discover the practices implicit in project stories, so you can make them explicit and reveal behaviours that contribute to either sleepwalking or sparke for individuals and teams.

During Practice Spotting™, there are some elements you should look for in project stories to help in recording a Practice Card:

- Storyteller's behaviours which is important if the storyteller is a character in the story.
- Characters in the story, including the storyteller if relevant.
- Feelings, body language and emotions at play.
- Behaviours of people as they interact with each other during the story.
- How people in the story treat each other.
- Where the story took place.
- Environmental conditions in that place.
- Storyteller's language and tone.
- Outcomes of or actions in the story.

Barriers to deeper understanding of people include:

- Incorrectly making assumptions about what other people need, who they are, what they do or what type of people they are.
- Gaps in relationships during which we do not speak to one another.

Tools to Make Meaningful Work

- Deadlines that lead to having little time for reflecting on stories and the relationships and practices within those stories.

- Lacking a space for connecting the data that already exists in different parts of an organization to gain a clearer understanding of needs.

- Lacking the time to set priorities, see the path ahead and plan your work because we are constantly focusing on tasks that meet short-term goals and implementing them quickly.

Applying Practice Spotting™

Practice Spotting™ allows you to look more broadly and deeply into what was happening in the interactions and relationships between the people and places across different moments in time. Practice Spotting™ can be used:

- To unlock implicit or unseen behaviours and make them explicit.

- To observe, make sense, reflect and break down behavioural patterns.

- To gain multiple perspectives.

- To help us understand the grand narratives and patterns.

Practice Spotting™ can also be used:

- As a key that you can insert into environments consisting of people, time, place and practices.

- To go deeper into layers that we may not have seen immediately.

- To unlock implicit or unseen practices and make these explicit.

- As a way to observe, make sense of, reflect and break down behavioural patterns.

- To gain multiple perspectives.

- For intersecting meaningful moments.

When using Practice Spotting™ remember the following:

- There is no right or wrong way.

- There is no static environment that exists because change is fluid and flows across people, time and place.

- There is no formula because we see varied practices that have different dimensions, environments and contexts.

- Different people in different times can spot different practices and you may spot different practices when you do Practice Spotting™ on the same story at different times.

- There is always something to see across the layers and Practice Spotting™ can feel like peeling an onion one layer at a time.

- Usually, implicit practices lie under the surface and are hidden.

- Discovering a practice requires that you perceive its multiple parts, including yourself and the environment in which you work.

Practice Spotting™ can give you the opportunity to thrive. It leads you to practice with another person and to reflect individually and together. This serves as a reminder to find the people, time and place to reflect on what practices matter and to record practices in your Make Meaningful Work Guided Practice Journal.

7 steps to do Practice Spotting™

Practice Spotting™ is a tool that helps us to widen our perspectives and dig deeper into what we see on the surface. It enables us to be more aware of implicit practices. It also allows us to turn words into actions by creating Practice Cards in connection with your context to practice on a daily basis, preferably with a practice buddy.

The 7 steps to do Practice Spotting™ are as follows:

step1
Identify a unit of analysis

Practice Spotting™ requires a unit of analysis. We refer to the primary unit of analysis as a project story. Other units of analysis include the following:

- Stories at work – we often start here.
- Scenarios – these are the situations that people are currently facing.
- Conversations – you can use any conversation to get started doing Practice Spotting™.
- People – these are the people with whom you are interacting.

- Learning events – these are the teachable moments you are experiencing.

- Articles, films, documentaries and books – resources give you the opportunity to learn from the experiences of others.

Each unit of analysis has within it certain characteristics that help you observe, unpack, and understand what's happening within and around you. In Practice Spotting™ you will use these units of analysis in observing and clarifying the conversations, language, and emotions that occur between people. You can practice spot a high level story or a particular moment in a story.

step2
Use relevant lenses

Practice Spotting™ uses multiple lenses to help us advance potential and widen perspectives. It helps us see, feel, sense, hear and consider blind spots and biases in our interactions and relationships with others.

As people collaborate together, these lenses might focus on motivations, power, body language, emotions, energies, attitudes, language or tone. Encouraging organizations to take enough time for structured explicit reflection and pursue ideas or practices that pique their curiosity following these four lenses:

1. Attitude and mindset – open or closed.
2. Perspectives and opportunities – past, present and future.
3. Communication and intent – individual and team outcomes.
4. Impact and time – success based on commitment.

We use these lenses to:

- See from other perspectives.
- Broaden horizons.
- See where our own views fit with others.
- Add diversity.
- Expand our knowledge.

There are no right or wrong lenses. You can use the lenses you need in the specific context to gain the perspectives required to make more meaningful decisions. These Practice Spotting™ lenses help you understand different dimensions of your work. More explicitly, it allows you to sense, spot and understand the practices around the interactions and relationships between people.

step3
Practice Spotting™ explicit and implicit practices

Let's start with this question first:

What is explicitly or implicitly happening or not happening between people?

Explicit or seen practices

You will derive your practices through Practice Spotting™ and make them explicit by recording them on a Practice Card. You will adopt these explicit practices and engage in continuous learning with your colleagues at work.

Explicit practices are above the surface and most of the time are transactional activities such as the tasks we need to do, processes we need to follow, outputs we need to deliver or KPIs we have to meet.

Implicit or unseen practices

Implicit Practices are complex and multi-layered. They are in play constantly and continuously in our interactions and relationships with people. These Implicit Practices are harder to notice. They include values, beliefs, mindset, attitudes, soft skills, motivations and underlying behaviours and outcomes. We acquire most of these Implicit Practices without always acknowledging them, and we also use these Implicit Practices unconsciously.

Some of these Implicit Practices can have positive or negative impact on people. Since the smallest of behaviours can have a big impact on people, we need to pay more attention to these behaviours. We have to be aware of our Implicit Practices and that of others.

These practices are present in our day-to-day work and interactions with people. We call these implicit practices because we do not call out or record such practices. We also might not practice them on our own or with others.

Practice Spotting™ is a way of acquiring knowledge about what is really happening under the surface from both positive and negative perspectives.

step4
Write a Practice Card to connect and contextualize

Writing a Practice Card is one of the key activities in Make Meaningful Work. In traditional learning, we are given exercises to complete that usually do not relate to your own context and needs.

In Make Meaningful Work, you need to come up with your own contextualised micro exercises and an outcome that is relevant to you. So these contextual micro exercises are useful, practical and relevant to your needs and context.

A micro exercise can be something that you are already doing that you can do differently or improve upon and it should not take too much energy and time. Say for example, the practice you select is to show gratitude. An example contextual micro exercise you come up with is saying thank you followed up with a specific action e.g. "thank you for delivering the report on time" versus just saying thank you. Write the micro exercise, saying thank you followed with a specific action on your practice card.

When you create a Practice Card, you need to select a practice that you feel is relevant and connected to your context. The Practices you select could be:

- Something you are already proficient in that you would like to enhance.
- A practice gap that needs to be improved.
- A new practice that you would like to pay more attention to.

Practice Spotting™ lets us catalog and extract these elements so we can convert them into useful understanding. This helps us to identify and extract a practice which then becomes a Practice Card.

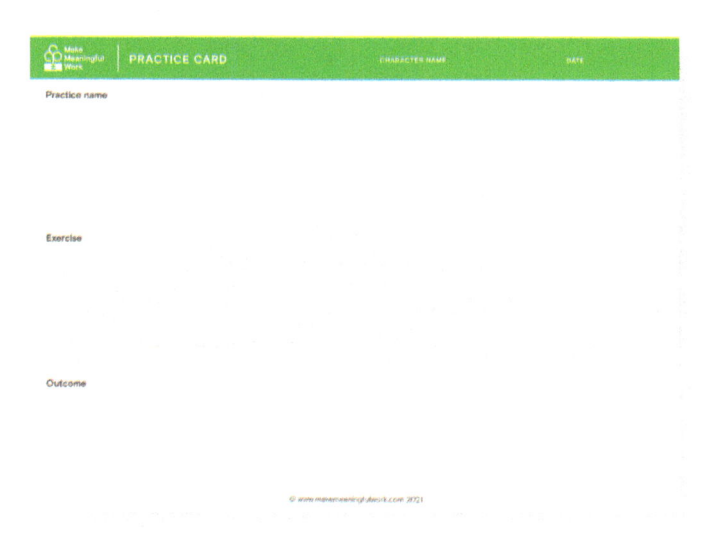

step5
Take ownership, practice and track progress

Pairing with another person and gaining a diverse set of backgrounds and perspectives is key to optimal practice. We often learn more from others with a different point of view who can then offer us experiences we may not have been exposed to previously.

Pairing implies that we take the time to be present with another person and explicitly call out and practice some practices together.

After practicing, take the time to develop structured explicit reflection on what you have observed, and experienced and where we require additional practice. This pairing also allows us to discover new or related practices that we may need, depending on how we wish to develop individually and together.

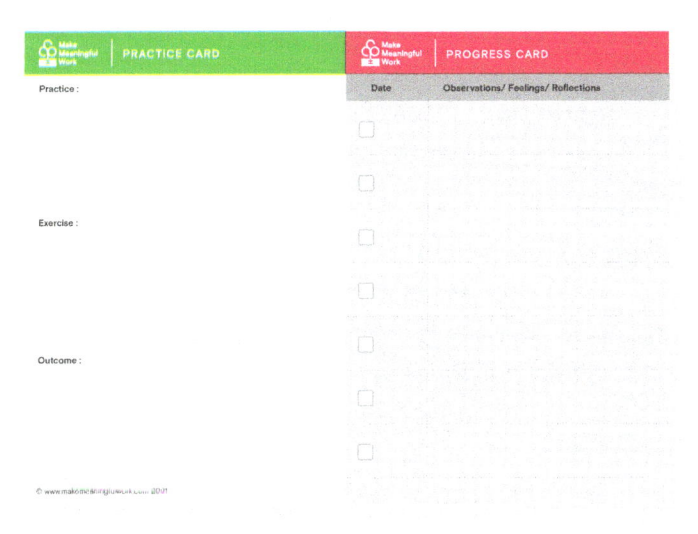

PRACTICE CARD		PROGRESS CARD	
Practice :		Date	Observations/ Feelings/ Reflections
		☐	
		☐	
Exercise :		☐	
		☐	
Outcome :		☐	
		☐	
		☐	

© www.makemeaningfulwork.com 2021

step6
Reflect with a buddy

The Make Meaningful Work Guided Practice Journal helps to record, reflect and track progress of your practice and learnings. To create moments for structured explicit reflection and practice, do the following:

1. **Choose a practice** – apply practices from the Practice Cards that are relevant to solving the problem.

2. **Consider the contextual micro exercises-** consider what contextual mico exercises you might do that would be relevant to and have sustained relevance across different scenarios. The primary driver should be the ability to repeat the exercise to gain depth of practice and reflect on the learning outcomes.

3. **Find someone to practice with-** choose people who can help you do specific exercises and use specific practices together. Who you choose is important because it helps you understand who you like learning with. It also lets you know which specific practices different practice buddies can help you confront and address over time. This enables you to gain depth of practice and reflect on your learning outcomes.

4. **Put the practice into practice.** Practicing a practice can take as little as one or two minutes for a more structured process.

5. **Reflect on your learning outcomes.** Integrate your new learnings into your practice card library.

step7
Get support and support others in the global "Meaning Maker Community"

As you take more time to practice with others, you will also discover specific practices that you need to sharpen over time. These specific practices may require the experience of people who can facilitate this and make it real. Facilitators give you someone to turn to in order to provide the support you need, which is based on both individual and team requirements.

Practice Spotting™ in Action

Bruno Fernenades is a Manchester United football player and in an interview, he was describing how he took a free kick in a derby game in early 2020.

In this example and in a matter of 20 seconds of game time, Bruno demonstrates both amazing leadership and football skills.

He was able to "connect and contextualise" his soft skills to help his team score a goal.

Story Card

| STORY CARD | CHARACTER NAME: Amy |

Story Name: **Bruno taking free kick**

Watch Video

Here's the transcript of the video:

"I start talking with Fred because normally we talk, we will take, we will take right. And was H in the area and say, left foot is better for us for attacking the ball. And I start talking, I already saw, uh, Anton, look at me, he looks at me. I look at him. I, I feel he wants the same of me. So you go for feelings, you know, maybe I, I will put the ball in. Sometimes Anto don't go. And then, that moment I stopped, I talked with Fred and I talked like, okay, Fred, you go for, for, for maybe, you know, if someone of Manchester City listen or everything, they start, okay. He tells Fred go. So we can relax For example, on the wall was Aguero on this side, Gündoğan I think, and maybe when they saw Fred going back and me on the ball, they think, okay, Fred goes and they relax a little bit. And I start to look for H and start like go second post go second post. And in the moment the referee whistle, I feel Anto ready, I feel Anto, just I go now and I have the right time, was the perfect ball, it was the perfect finish. Was everything in the right time, you know, but sometimes we will miss, we will miss, but we try, we need to try because it was a difficult ball, but I try and we score."

Practice Spotting™ the clip

Amy watched the clip and inspired her to do Practice Spotting™ and wants to sense the environment in meeting rooms like Bruno was able to do during the match.

Here's a Spotting Card to demonstrate the explicit practice Amy sees and the depth of implicit practices that are in play:

Spotting Card

| SPOTTING CARD | CHARACTER NAME: Amy |

Story Name: **Bruno taking free kick**

Explicit Practice

- Taking free-kick
- Follow rules
- Listen out for whistles of Referee

Implicit Practice

- Taking leadership proactively in a stressful time (courageous)
- Feeling, Sensing teams & environment in the moment
- Form strategies fast and execute
- Adapt according to context
- Collaborate & take ownership making decision
- Demo "give it a try" spirit
- Take responsibility
- Confront & facing difficult decision
- Build team spirit

Practice Card

🌱 | PRACTICE CARD　　　　**CHARACTER NAME: Amy**

Practice Name :

Sensing
- Understand more about what others do & where they come from.

Exercise :

Week 1: Go to meetings early and observe people coming into the room.

Week 2: Go to meetings early and speak to people.

Week 3: Talk to people coming to the meetings 1-2 days before the meeting.

Outcome :

Understand more about what others do & where they come from.

Make Meaningful Work Guided Practice Journal Tool

"The MMW Guided Practice Journal acts as a facilitator that creates explicit prompts opening up opportunities for structured reflective habits. The journal also encourages deeper and thoughtful performance reviews to leapfrog over major roadblocks and sustain healthy practices."

Derek Black

The Make Meaningful Work Guided Practice Journal is a light tool that provides a structure to observe, reflect and record.

The Make Meaningful Work Guided Practice Journal records observations and provides explicit moments at which to stop, be present, reflect on and record what you have learned as a result of the experience of working with others.

The practice of keeping a journal helps us to:

- Gain a much clearer understanding of ourselves.
- Experience how an open and safe workspace feels like.
- Acquire a deeper understanding of the people with whom we are working with.

- Develop practical methods (in the form of practice cards) that help us learn and apply these practices.

- Connect with others who may have interests in similar topics, practices, or themes.

- Continue to apply practices you feel strongly about.

- Understand capability gaps and what is needed to enhance and improve them

Journaling instruments

(ⓘ Refer to Appendix)

Here are some extracts from the important instruments from the Make Meaningful Work Guided Practice Journal. We will continue to update the journal.

Create a learning and development environment to record, reflect, aggregate, check progress and sustain meaningful practices as follows:

Roles and Responsibilities Map
This helps you to see the connections between the roles that you play in different contexts and the values and outcomes you seek. It also identifies the character traits and practices relevant to you and any practice gaps you may need to address over time. This helps to provide an overview of yourself and who you work with.

It also helps us explore our being (where we are now) and our becoming (what lies ahead).

Character Card

The primary goal of creating a Character Card is to help you build your character so that you see yourself clearly. Understanding your character helps you better understand yourself and the people with whom you work.

Creating Character Cards helps you reflect on what you have learned. It refines your understanding of what matters to you and your team and why it matters. You can use these Character Cards to understand the character of who you practice with and see multiple dimensions of people through the use of stories.

The Character Card is not intended to box you into specific character types, rather this is to open up and enhance your character traits and reactivate your potential.

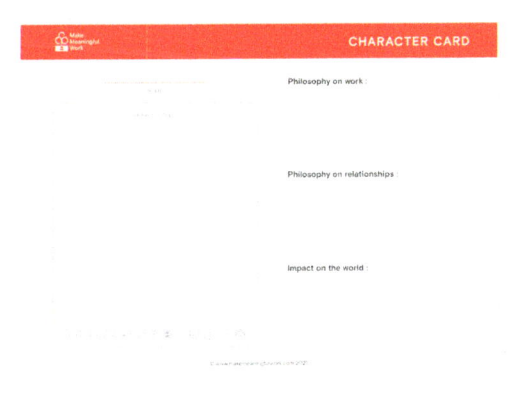

Story Cards

Story Cards help record the unit of analysis to use with Practice Spotting™. We need a place to record stories as a story can develop further over time. One story can spot many different explicit and implicit practices when you consider it at different times. A story can provide different perspectives through different lenses such as people, time and place. You do not need to be a great writer to record a story; it can be a specific moment that triggers a memory and has an impact for you. This is also a place to record the development of the story and include references.

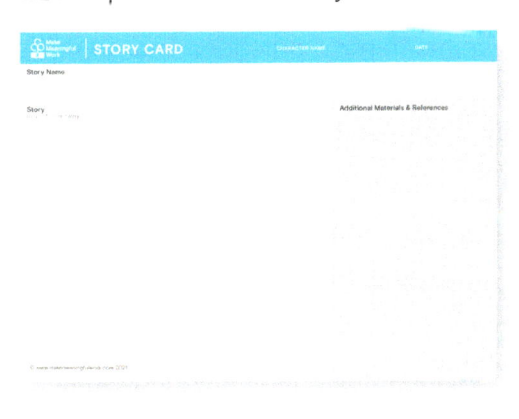

Notes Cards

Notes Cards are used to make more structured notes as you listen to stories and record keywords or key practices that you observe. You may also transfer these notes onto the Spotting Cards as you summarise your thoughts. You can consider the key practices relevant to your own situation so that you connect and contextualise the practices to derive meaningful outcomes.

Spotting Cards

Spotting Cards help you take the key observations from the Notes and Story Cards. It also helps you apply lenses to spot the meaningful practices and outcomes that can connect and contextualise what you do. We apply lenses on the practice we choose to break down.

Start with the Explicit Practices observed. Explore and outline the Implicit Practices that are under the soil on the left of the tree diagram. It takes time and practice to observe the Implicit

Practices. Remember that there are no right or wrong answers. Pick an Implicit Practice from under the soil on the left and write this on the top of the right side of the card. Start to break this down further to explore deeper using the enablers and barriers lenses.

Practice Cards

A Practice Card describes a practice, relevant exercises and behavioural benefits that can result from adopting a practice individually or as a team. Practice Cards inform what practices you wish to learn and apply, as well as those that you need to stop. Practices are derived from the stories and have sustained value. Practice Cards also reveal people who are particularly interested in specific practices and who can become practice leads.

As you continue Practice Spotting™, you can create your own library of practice cards and over time, determine which cards are important for you and your team. You will define patterns that help you discover the values and beliefs that you want to embody in the environment in which you work. Practices improve capabilities and imply an explicit behavioural intention to improve and action.

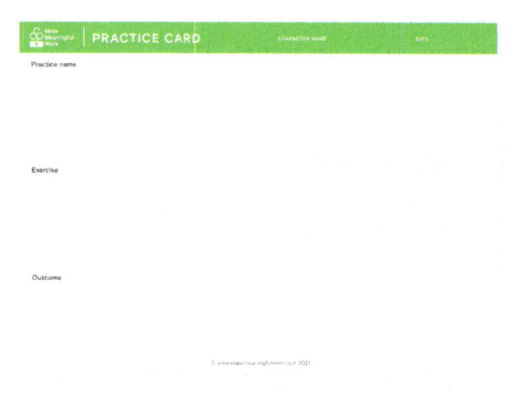

Practice & Progress Cards

Progress Cards help you track a specific practice, exercise and outcome over a period of time. This helps you record your observations, feelings and structured explicit reflections. It also determines if you are improving in that specific practice.

Learning Portfolio

The Learning Portfolio is used to collect all your structured explicit reflections. It also summarizes those practices and other topics you would like to learn and teach. Creating the portfolio helps you understand moments such as:

- **Learning** - creating continuous momentum or movement towards learning; promoting the idea that there is something to learn or refine every day.

- **Portfolio** - a record of the knowledge you have gained by investing in learning.

It might include items such as:

- **References or sources that interest you**— that you want to read, follow, learn from, or subscribe to.

- **Themes and gaps that** you have identified over time that may be important to you.

- **Topics** that you may want to write articles about.

- **Practices** that you would like to adopt individually or with learning buddies.

As you consider creating a Learning Portfolio for yourself and others, answer the following questions:

- What have we learned from our past interactions? The answer is: What you believe you have learned.

- What opportunities lie ahead for future learnings? The answer is: What you believe you don't know.

- Considering gaps relating to people, times, and places and who to learn from? The answer should include: people within and outside your circle that challenge your biases and assumptions and track continuous learning.

- What are the themes or topics that you would like to teach or share with others? This is the best way to enhance what you already know.

A Learning Portfolio can help you track the knowledge that you gain over time and see what practices you should spend your time on to continue learning. For some areas of learning, you will need to keep expanding your knowledge and connect it with other things you are learning. A Learning Portfolio provides a constant prompt that guides continuous, life-long learning.

Meaning Canvas

This is a place to define what is meaningful. It also determines the people, places and practices that matter to you and the community you work with, both inside and outside your work places. The intention of the canvas is to make some implicit practices explicit so we can shape the culture we desire.

The Meaning Canvas is a compliment to the Business Canvas for individuals and teams. It gives a summary of your values, goals, roles you want to play, concerns you have, recognition you want, feedback you want to address and the behaviours you want to model. It is a way for people to see what behaviours are expected and what behaviours are not tolerated.

Creating a Meaning Canvas lets you aggregate and summarize your learnings using the following:

- **Values** – internalize what values represent how you want to treat others and how you want them to treat you. Understanding these values also demonstrates your intentions and the related practices that embody them.

- **Mindset and attitude** – what we wish to encourage and discourage.

- **Behaviours and interactions** – decide what positive behaviours you want to encourage and what negative behaviours you want to avoid in the way you treat each other and yourself.

- **Goals** – what are you trying to achieve?

- **Actions** – to achieve the goals you set for yourself.

- **Recognition and rewards** – what you wish to celebrate and show gratitude for.

- **Feedback received** – feedback from others for your structured explicit reflections.

- **Practices needed** – identify what capabilities might be deficient. What practices do you need to enhance to help you do meaningful work?

The Meaning Canvas is a way to summarize what you have learned by using all our tools to refine the elements of what is meaningful to you and your team. The clues that let you refine meaning for you and your team are present in the project stories, as well as the Practice Spotting™ sessions you conduct on a regular basis. This helps you to create the practices that have meaning to you and your team.

Complimentary Online Learning Adventures using tools to Make Meaningful Work

Here is a complimentary Learning Adventure Card and practices you can try out for yourself:

> **Learning Adventure Card**
>
> **Identify risks towards new opportunities**
> - **Widen perspectives**
> - Aware of blindspots
> - Open minded

Take the online Learning Adventures here

ch. 00 01 02 **03**

03 sparkle studio

to sustain meaningful work

88   What is Sparkle Studio?
89   Sparkle Studio in action
91   Sustaining the Make Meaningful Work Sparkle Studio community
92   Ten behavioural outcomes from the Sparkle Studio
97   Multidisciplinary community
98   Join our Adventures ahead

What is Sparkle Studio?

Sparkle Studio is both physical and online and encapsulates a fun practice and learning experience. The Sparkle Studio is a simulation of a TV or radio show where team members play different roles to produce a show together. In that process, team members will:

- Get to know each other in a different setting in a cross and interdisciplinary manner.

- Have opportunities to learn from each other.

- Use the Make Meaningful Work tools to observe and practice the implicit practices that can be connected and contextualised into real work.

- Have a structured and explicit way to reflect together.

- Rehearse and set the culture the team wants.

Sparkle Studio in action

The MMW Sparkle Studio Kit includes the following to setup your own Sparkle Studio:

- Make Meaningful Work Sparkle Studio Playbook
- Instructional Videos
- Props

Here are some example scenarios to apply the Sparkle Studio in your own contexts at work:

01
Join a public studio

- Join the public Sparkle Studio Shows.
- Start with online self learning, practice and journaling.
- Find a learning buddy to practice and reflect with.

02
Setup your own studio with the MMW Sparkle Studio Kit

- Identify the core team members to facilitate and lead a studio.

- The MMW team will mentor the core team members on how to facilitate an accompanying program based on the outcomes and practices you need.

- Pair up buddies to practice and reflect on relevant outcomes and practices.

- Run the Sparkle Studio in different parts of an organisation regularly to promote interdisciplinary interactions, rehearse the culture you want, practice the practices according to the roles and outcomes you want to achieve together.

03
Plug-in the studio in different contexts

For example:

- Setting aside 15mins in weekly update meetings to share project stories where we can assign team members to do Practice Spotting™

- Setting moments to create Practice Cards during and after update meetings and start practicing micro exercises immediately.

- Where learnings and reflections become structured and explicit, and where practices and experiences are recorded to implement the practices right away. This illustrates that reflections can be easy and fun.

Sustaining the Make Meaningful Work Sparkle Studio community

Humans are social and communal beings. We are interdependent, want to feel valued and like to contribute to something beyond just ourselves. By running the Sparkle Studio regularly in different parts of the organization, it builds and supports a social and communal intention. We get to do structured and explicit reflections, rehearse and shape the culture we want and get the practices into the work environment right away.

In the Sparkle Studio community, we need to:

- Be more present, interested and aware during conversations.

- Give people undivided attention and help others to feel more at ease.

- Listen to hear what we are actually saying.

- Encourage better questions to gain a depth of understanding so as to inform meaningful decision making.

By encouraging all of us to practice and support each other in refining meaning for individuals, teams and the organisations you work in, we make our communities and the planet healthier.

10 Behavioural outcomes from the Sparkle Studio

The Sparkle Studio provides opportunities for experimentation and improvisation to explicitly express the culture you want to shape. When we are in a relaxed, energetic and fun environment, it makes the learning outcomes more effective.

The Sparkle Studio encourages the following ten behavioural outcomes:

1. Enable Active Listening
Active listening is fully concentrating on what is being said rather than just passively 'hearing' the message of the speaker and involves listening with all senses. Forming relationships with others means viewing them as our equals who can contribute actively to our conversations. In the Sparkle Studio, listening before speaking is very important to get the studio up and running. This allows us to better understand the person in an unfamiliar environment. Remember, you have two ears with which to practice listening.

2. Build Awareness
Building awareness helps to grow knowledge or perception of a situation or fact. The Sparkle Studio helps everyone become aware of biases using Practice Spotting™. It widens our

perspectives on the assumptions made by people about themselves and others. This is vital to our approach to solving problems.

3. Spark Curiosity

Curiosity is a strong desire to know or learn something. In the Sparkle Studio environment, there are many unfamiliar and interesting ways of operating and thinking. To learn and improve, we need to get out of our cubicles and understand other people. We must encourage individuals, teams and organisations to foster constant curiosity about how they can serve themselves and others better.

4. Solve Ambiguous Problems

Solving ambiguous problems requires a thinker who focuses on the problem as stated and tries to synthesize information and knowledge to achieve a solution. As goals in the Sparkle Studio need to be done in a relatively short period of time, issues can be confronted and resolved quickly. This is an opportunity for the Sparkle Studio to be more aware of any issues and address them professionally in a timely manner. We can then develop a plan and agree on a focus, as exploring this will determine the quality of the outcomes.

5. Foster Quality Relationships

Fostering a quality relationship involves trust, feeling of security and satisfaction. In the Sparkle Studio, goals and roles are clearly defined and trust is established throughout the studio efforts. We often perceive trust once it is already present. However, the way we build trust is often unconscious and instinctive. Our ability to build trust comes directly from our ability to be vulnerable and accept other ways of doing things. While it may sound counterintuitive, one way to start building trust and foster quality relationships between people is to start trusting others before you gain their trust.

6. Contextual Adaptability

Contextual adaptability is the quality of being able to adjust to new conditions. There are many unexpected incidents that can happen during the production of shows in the Sparkle Studio. Thinking on your feet and adapting to the situation is very important. When sharing stories in the Sparkle Studio, people come together, do Practice Spotting™ on stories and record practices on Practice Cards. These practices enable people to identify important moments that encourage breaking down the practices into more granular practices to connect and contextualise into your own work.

7. Promote Diversity

Diversity is a practice or quality of including or involving people from a range of different backgrounds, beliefs and perspectives. Sparkle Studio is multidisciplinary in nature; the crew and audience are made up of various people from different parts of the organisation. When we play various roles in the Sparkle Studio, goals become clear. We can then achieve them in a fun environment, taking ownership and responsibility naturally as people play different roles. In the Sparkle Studio, there are many roles a person can play that they may not be familiar with. By trying out new roles, we are pushing our boundaries, promoting diversity and forming new wiring in our brains.

8. Navigate Complexity

Navigating complexity is the ability to adjust to a changing environment or situation and to adopt a flexible approach that shifts according to the situation. In and outside of the Sparkle Studio, we are facing a complex world with many pathways to navigate. In the Sparkle Studio, you get opportunities to practice navigating complexity by trying our different roles. Some of these opportunities require improvisation in considering the problems and building strong relationships with others. Thinking on your feet implies unpacking the problems using different lenses. It also widens perspectives to better define possible meaningful outcomes. Sometimes, this can feel uncomfortable and unintuitive. However, these are often the best moments to learn from and to record as practices in Practice Cards, as it allows others to benefit when a similar situation repeats itself.

9. Build confidence

Confidence is the feeling or belief that one can have faith in or rely on someone or something. Making a Sparkle Studio show together focuses on collective achievement. It also gives you a chance to practice the Implicit Practices that you are good at or want to enhance. Collective achievement boosts confidence immediately and enhances the practices to build confidence over time.

10. Make Meaningful Decisions

To make a meaningful decision implies a serious, important, useful, constructive and sustainable outcome. In the Sparkle Studio, participants do not just learn the words; they need to take actions and make timely and meaningful decisions on the spot with the variety of roles they need to play. The Implicit Practices they build are transferable to the decisions they need to make in their work environment. The Sparkle Studio is an ongoing practice that encourages a cross disciplinary, long term, strategic and collective thinking mindset.

Multidisciplinary community

When we focus on Implicit Practices (transferable soft skills), it does not matter which department you come from as this is applicable to everyone. The Sparkle Studio becomes the hub and catalyst for multidisciplinary communication and understanding. It forms a sustaining community.

Join Our Adventures ahead ⎯⎯⎯⎯⎯⎯⎯⎯⎯⎯

We would like to thank you for being part of our adventure towards moving from Sleepwalking to a Sparkle future where we can all insert meaning into what we do. This is a difficult task we are giving to ourselves, but we will continue to grow our learnings and the global community. We hope you will continue to contribute and be a part of Make Meaningful Work Adventures together with the global community.

We hope to see you in Make Meaningful Work shows, events and Learning Adventures.

Complimentary Online Learning Adventures to apply and sustain meaningful work

Here is a complimentary Learning Adventure Card and practices you can try out for yourself:

> **Learning Adventure Card**
>
> Encourage respect and inclusivity to build trust
>
> - **Encourage respect**
> - Being Inclusive
> - Being trustworthy

Take the online Learning Adventures here

How Make Meaningful Work has helped you?

Here are some quotes from people who have applied Make Meaningful Work and how it has helped them.

"MMW is a series of learning adventures that enables us to focus our energy on understanding more about our character, and building and sustaining healthy cultures. It's anchored to a community and studio experience that provides the support and tools to be reflective and establishes sustained practices relative to an individual's role. For me, the real sweet spot has been plugging in the MMW framework to our employee development cycle. As a result, their growth and development have become more meaningful and it has created a foundation to widen perspectives and foster strong relationships. Providing positive client outcomes is essential and what helps us achieve this is creating the space for people to pause and engage in deeper reflective learning and development. The team is using language in their everyday interactions like "practice spotting" and "journaling" which demonstrates the sustained mindset they have towards the MMW tools."

Kim, Practice Lead, New Zealand

"MMW is a diverse global community of people I connect with to enjoy and create learning experiences. MMW challenges me to reflect on my actions, take practical steps to improve, and look for new possibilities. MMW is all about truly, meaningful decision making in whatever you do, and this resonates with me as a person, a parent and a leader at work."

Aaron, Senior Risk Partner, Australia

"MMW is all about making space... making space to reflect with others, making space to get outside of your usual bubble, making space to think big and think small, making space to connect the dots, making space to always get better."

Susan, Principal, USA/Australia

"Looking at MMW through the lens of a designer, I see immediate benefits: identifying practices that benefit both cultural dynamics as well as the manner in which we create. Developing (our own personal) narrative. Leveraging our personal system of values to look beyond ourselves, toward the betterment of others and the environment. That said, the program's extensibility is where its beauty lies; it's not just of value for the designer, of course, but for the project manager. Or the dentist. Or the librarian. As such, in the DNA of the program is an inclusive experience agnostic of role, industry, or hierarchical position in an org chart. Exploring the innate valuable practices that are implicit in everything we do, and projecting them outward—making them explicit—enables us, those around us, to understand and leverage their value. Yes, it's about our own evolution, but that evolution is also bigger than us—to what we create, how we create it, and to those on the receiving end of it all. And for me—a servant leader driven by humble respect—being mindful of the bigger picture is what it's all about. The designer's legacy isn't built upon their choice of tools; the designer's legacy is built upon the choices they make—as macro and micro as that implies."

Justin, Vice President, Design, USA

"MMW charged up my brain and rewired my thinking on how I should lead my team to constructively challenge the status quo and grow ourselves ready for any challenges"

Richard, Head of Digital, China

"What I have found with MMW are two things of immense value to me:

1. MMW is an intuitive and challenging process that provides me with personally relevant learning every time that I choose to engage. It's beautifully designed. The intentionality of it's "human" approach means that every individual can learn. MMW doesn't confine me with structural limitations and is instead engineered to foster the unparalleled ability of self-directed learning.

2. MMW provides me with a community, outside of my narrow professional field that can share insight that is uncommon, diverse and fortified with experience from a variety of perspectives and industries. It consistently provides high calibre people with the best of intentions for their own growth and for that of the others in the group."

Greg, Executive Director, USA

"MMW is to me a Bold Intent. We do not strive to explain the work we do today as meaningful, to do it more fun-ly, or even more impactfully. Rather, we intend to make meaningful work, even and especially when that necessitates stopping work which is pointless or harmful. We intend to unite and enrol those we choose to surround ourselves with, and to MAKE meaningful change, together."

Andrew, CEO, New Zealand

"MMW helped me understand the underlying themes in my development as a person and a manager, to more consciously create a positive environment for others, and to connect with some amazing like-minded people. Huge love and thanks to Dan & Jo and the rest of the MMW community for bringing us all more optimism and confidence in making meaningful work in the world."

Kathryn, Research Manager, USA

"The Make Meaningful Work approach and thinking that Dan and Jo developed have helped our team to realise that learning to become a better professional in design research goes beyond learning the research and design skills they expected. MMW gives lots of attention to skills that are more general and hard to describe, such as listening, bringing yourself into your work, being authentic, developing your voice, being brave at work, dealing with difficult topics, and so on. It changed our perspective on what should be at the centre of our learning and development programme, and helped us to make that transition work."

Bas, Creative Director, The Netherlands/UK

"A job ensures livelihood. A career might be a passion. A vocation is personally meaningful. Make Meaningful Work is a timely initiative to enable all of us to ponder the greater meaning of what we do at work, putting things into action to create better working cultures as well as shaping our personal growth"

Keith Tam, Designer and Educator, China

"MMW is a very personal journey of self discovery. It helped me reconnect to the core values I believe in and learn how to practice these values consistently. Eventually this has become my brand, my unique story. When we care, we want to make things work, meaningfully and impactfully. To connect yourself with the people you care about and things that you value to contextualize and to practice. It helps to get things done with Sparkle and that's what MMW means to me"

Koni, Financial Risk and Governance Manager, China

"MMW is: a way to look more closely, stop sleepwalking, and act accordingly"

Andrea, Information Architect, Sweden

"How do we confront our past? Without dwelling on it but to move forward? How do we create space to reflect in the busy moments? I've found that through the MMW dialogue, grounding my understanding of self, character and identity, this has helped find personal meaning and navigate my own learning journey to better integrate my beliefs, passions and impact I would like to have on the larger whole"

Michael Ong, Product Team Coach, Singapore

"Instead of just a flavour in the mouth, MMW provides a sustainable framework that helped me progressively cultivate a team where every member can discover the true meaning of work"

Pru, Head of FinBiz Development, China

"Dan and Jo have come up with a fresh, innovative and fun approach to helping with work culture. A positive and productive employee experience is one of the biggest priorities that organisations have now! The problem is that management's traditional command and control methods to connect with staff are no longer relevant or authentic. This is where MMW comes in. Focusing on "the person" and looking beyond the transactional to the emotional, they have a genuinely human-centred practice. Lovely!"

Dave, CEO, UK

"MMW creates a healthy distance needed to use feedback loops to record, reflect, practice and sustain contextually relevant transferable soft skills. It helps me take ownership of the practices and insert meaning into what I do for myself and others and codify both the successes and learnings in work cultures."

Derek, Educator, China

"When my father was alive, he told me that he was happy with me as long as I found meaning in my work and life. He was absolutely right. It is vital to your own well being and happiness to find meaning in what you do. Not only does MMW help you identify and achieve that, it also sustains your positive feelings, thoughts and actions in the long term. May we all insert meaning in our work and life"

Jin, Teacher/Author, UAE

appendix
Journaling Instruments

Extracts from the
Make Meaningful Work
Guided Practice Journal.

ROLES & RESPONSIBILITIES MAP

Context	Roles = Responsibilities	Values	Character Traits	Practices
Individual	Family Friends			
Organization	Team Department Co-worker	Outcomes		
Industry				
Society				
Planet				

© www.makemeaningfulwork.com 2021

CHARACTER CARD

NAME

DRAW YOURSELF

Philosophy on work :

Philosophy on relationships :

Impact on the world :

© www.makemeaningfulwork.com 2021

Make Meaningful Work | **STORY CARD** | CHARACTER NAME | DATE

Story Name

Story
Record down your story

Additional Materials & References

© www.makemeaningfulwork.com 2021

NOTES

CHARACTER NAME

DATE

2. Key Practices / Key Words

1. Notes from stories

3. Summary of your thoughts

© www.makemeaningfulwork.com 2021

SPOTTING CARD

CHARACTER NAME

DATE

Explicit Practices

Break down a Practice

Enablers

Barriers

Implicit Practices

© www.makemeaningfulwork.com 2021

PRACTICE CARD

CHARACTER NAME

DATE

Practice name

Exercise

Outcome

© www.makemeaningfulwork.com 2021

PROGRESS CARD

Date	Observations/ Feelings/ Reflections
☐	
☐	
☐	
☐	
☐	
☐	
☐	

© www.makemeaningfulwork.com 2021

PRACTICE CARD

Practice :

Exercise :

Outcome :

Make Meaningful Work | **LEARNING PORTFOLIO**

DATE — **CHARACTER NAME**

What am I learning/making/doing?

Would like to teach / share with others

© www.makemeaningfulwork.com 2021

MEANING CANVAS

TEAM NAME

DATE

Communicate, plan, and support each other. Let's work together how to become a meaningful team.

Values	Mindset & Attitude	Behaviours & Interactions	Goals
	Encourage / Discourage	Encourage / Discourage	

Actions	Recognition & Rewards	Feedback Received	Practices Needed

Make Meaningful Work

© www.makemeaningfulwork.com 2021

About the authors

Josephine Wong

Jo is a co-founder and principal at Apogee (founded in 1997). She is also a co-founder of Make Meaningful Work and User Experience Hong Kong (both founded in 2010).

Jo grew up in multicultural Hong Kong with a Chinese-Burmese father and Chinese-Indonesian mother. She collaborates with global teams conducting research in Cantonese, Mandarin and English.

Jo is passionate about a sustainable environment, political and economic systems and how we can live healthier and meaningful lives without adversely impacting those less fortunate.

CHARACTER CARD

Jobot

Philosophy on work : Human beings are capable of creating good and bad outcomes. if we are not healthy both physically and mentally, our decisions e.g. choosing a job would not be suitable. If we are not happy at our work, we are creating lots of waste, wasting our time and resources in organisations, society and the planet.

Philosophy on relationships : Relationships are built on mutual respect whether its people relationships, animals or nature. People are not born equal, but we can treat others like equals and this can bring us more care and empathy about others.

Impact on the world : I would like to reduce tangible and intangible waste for myself and others. Get people to be more aware of the small things they do daily so they can insert positive energy into the interactions and relationships they have.

Daniel Szuc

Dan is a co-founder and principal at Apogee (founded in 1997). He is also co-founder of Make Meaningful Work and User Experience Hong Kong (both founded in 2010).

For over 20 years, he has been based in Hong Kong and has been involved in the User Experience field for 25 years. Dan promotes User Experience globally. He has co-authored two books : "Global UX" with Whitney Quesenbery and "The Usability Kit" with Gerry Gaffney.

MMW | Apogeehk | Books

CHARACTER CARD

Daniel Szuc

Philosophy on work :
- Be determined in what you do and work hard
- Read to improve on topics you do not know about
- Surround yourself with smart people who can challenge your perspectives

Philosophy on relationships :
- Be honest with yourself and others
  Share stories and learnings that can help other people
- Share knowledge and build community as a result

Impact on the world :
- Make people laugh and comfortable with themselves
- Help people express themselves
- Insert meaning in what you do